BY THOMAS K. ADAMSON

THE JACKSONVILLE

JAGUARS

STORY

TORQUE™

BELLWETHER MEDIA · MINNEAPOLIS, MN

Are you ready to take it to the extreme? Torque books thrust you into the action-packed world of sports, vehicles, mystery, and adventure. These books may include dirt, smoke, fire, and chilling tales. **WARNING**: read at your own risk.

This edition first published in 2017 by Bellwether Media, Inc.

No part of this publication may be reproduced in whole or in part without written permission of the publisher. For information regarding permission, write to Bellwether Media, Inc., Attention: Permissions Department, 5357 Penn Avenue South, Minneapolis, MN 55419.

Library of Congress Cataloging-in-Publication Data

Names: Adamson, Thomas K., 1970-
Title: The Jacksonville Jaguars Story / by Thomas K. Adamson.
Description: Minneapolis, MN : Bellwether Media, Inc., 2017. | Series:
    Torque: NFL Teams | Includes bibliographical references and index. |
    Audience: Ages: 7-12. | Audience: Grades: 3 through 7.
Identifiers: LCCN 2016007750 | ISBN 9781626173699 (hardcover : alk. paper)
Subjects: LCSH: Jacksonville Jaguars (Football team)–History–Juvenile literature.
Classification: LCC GV956.J33 .A38 2017 | DDC 796.332/6409759/12–dc23
LC record available at http://lccn.loc.gov/2016007750

Printed in the United States of America, North Mankato, MN.

TABLE OF CONTENTS

On November 30, 2014, the Jaguars trail the New York Giants 21 to 0. The Jaguars finally come alive in the second half. They cut the Giants' lead to only five points.

Marqise Lee

The Giants make a good pass play. But they
fumble! The Jaguars' Aaron Colvin picks
up the loose ball. He runs into the end zone.
Jacksonville takes the lead!

Josh Scobee

The Giants take back the lead with a field goal. In the final 30 seconds of the game, the Jaguars try a field goal. It is good!

The Jaguars stop New York's last scoring attempt with a **sack** and another fumble. The Jaguars recover the ball and the game is over. It is the biggest comeback win in team history!

SCORING TERMS

END ZONE

the area at each end of a football field; a team scores by entering the opponent's end zone with the football.

EXTRA POINT

a score that occurs when a kicker kicks the ball between the opponent's goal posts after a touchdown is scored; 1 point.

FIELD GOAL

a score that occurs when a kicker kicks the ball between the opponent's goal posts; 3 points.

SAFETY

a score that occurs when a player on offense is tackled behind his own goal line; 2 points for defense.

TOUCHDOWN

a score that occurs when a team crosses into its opponent's end zone with the football; 6 points.

TWO-POINT CONVERSION

a score that occurs when a team crosses into its opponent's end zone with the football after scoring a touchdown; 2 points.

The Jacksonville Jaguars were one of two **expansion teams** to first play in the National Football League (NFL) in 1995. In their first five seasons, they made the **playoffs** four times.

1995 season

AFC CHAMPIONSHIP
JANUARY 23, 2000

They also played in
two American Football
Conference (AFC)
Championship games.

The Jaguars play their home games at EverBank Field in Jacksonville, Florida. It opened in 1995 for their first season.

EverBank was one of the fastest NFL stadiums built. It only took about 19 months to tear down the old stadium and build a new one.

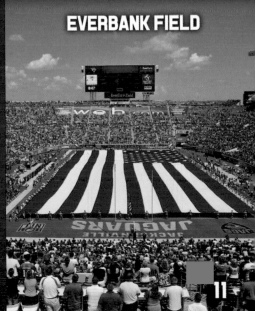

EVERBANK FIELD

JACKSONVILLE,
FLORIDA

N
W + E
S

In the AFC South **Division**, the Tennessee Titans are Jacksonville's main **rival**. The Jaguars' first-ever win was against the Titans (then called the Houston Oilers) in 1995. Jacksonville has gone head to head with Tennessee more than with any other team.

NFL DIVISIONS

 AFC

NORTH

 BALTIMORE **RAVENS**

 CINCINNATI **BENGALS**

 CLEVELAND **BROWNS**

 PITTSBURGH **STEELERS**

EAST

BUFFALO **BILLS**

 MIAMI **DOLPHINS**

PATRIOTS

 NEW YORK **JETS**

SOUTH

 TEXANS

 INDIANAPOLIS **COLTS**

 JACKSONVILLE **JAGUARS**

 TENNESSEE **TITANS**

WEST

DENVER **BRONCOS**

 CHIEFS

 RAIDERS OAKLAND **RAIDERS**

 SAN DIEGO **CHARGERS**

NFC

NFC NORTH

 CHICAGO
BEARS

 DETROIT
LIONS

 GREEN BAY
PACKERS

 MINNESOTA
VIKINGS

NFC EAST

DALLAS
COWBOYS

NEW YORK
GIANTS

 PHILADELPHIA
EAGLES

 WASHINGTON
REDSKINS

NFC SOUTH

 ATLANTA
FALCONS

 CAROLINA
PANTHERS

 NEW ORLEANS
SAINTS

 TAMPA BAY
BUCCANEERS

NFC WEST

 ARIZONA
CARDINALS

 LOS ANGELES
RAMS

 SAN FRANCISCO
49ERS

 SEATTLE
SEAHAWKS

A 1991 contest resulted in a name for Jacksonville's team before the expansion was even awarded.

1995 season

14

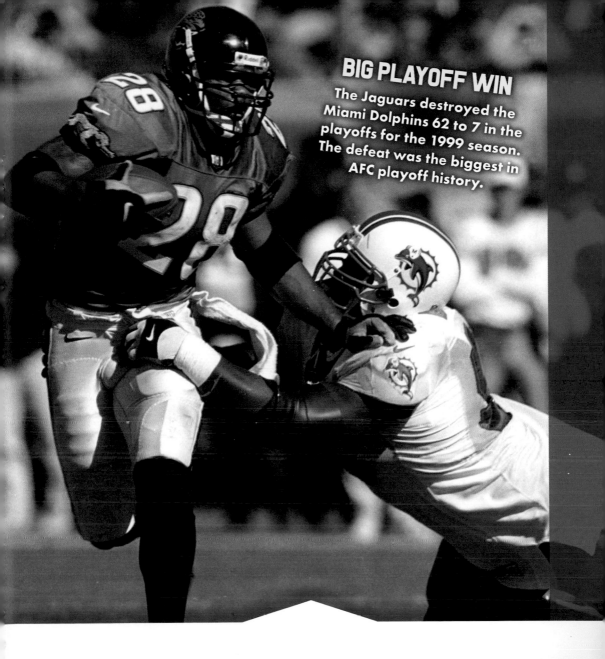

BIG PLAYOFF WIN

The Jaguars destroyed the Miami Dolphins 62 to 7 in the playoffs for the 1999 season. The defeat was the biggest in AFC playoff history.

Once the Jaguars eventually took the field in 1995, the team thrilled fans. They played fiercely in the AFC Central Division. In 2002, the Jaguars moved to the AFC South.

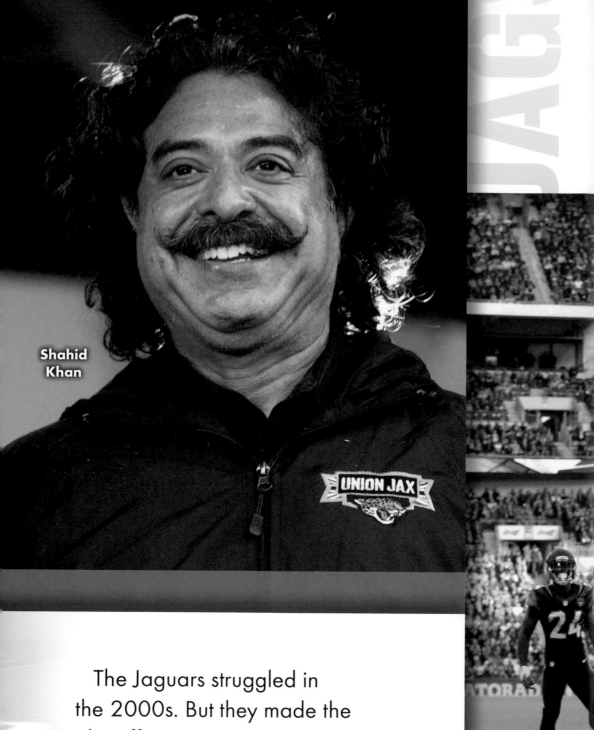

Shahid Khan

The Jaguars struggled in the 2000s. But they made the playoffs twice. In 2012, Shahid Khan became the team's owner.

More changes came in 2013 with a new head coach, Gus Bradley. Under new leadership, the Jaguars are working hard to win!

FANS ACROSS THE OCEAN

Khan increased the Jaguars' fan base in 2012. He arranged for the Jaguars to play once a year in London, England. Fans there are part of the Union Jax Fan Club!

JAGUARS

TIMELINE

1993

Awarded to Jacksonville as an NFL expansion team

1995

Played first regular season game in new stadium

1996

Played in first-ever playoff game, beating the Buffalo Bills

30 FINAL SCORE **27**

1995

Traded for quarterback Mark Brunell and drafted tackle Tony Boselli

1997

Made it to the playoffs for the second year in a row, but lost to the Denver Broncos

17 FINAL SCORE **42**

2012

Now owned by Shahid Khan

1998

Drafted running back
Fred Taylor

2000

Played in the AFC
Championship game
for the 1999 season

2014

Drafted wide receiver
Allen Robinson

2002

Moved to AFC South

2013

Played in London,
England, at Wembley
Stadium for the first time

2006

Drafted running back
Maurice Jones-Drew

JAGUARS

The Jaguars' first **quarterback** was Mark Brunell. He led the team to two AFC Championship games. Brunell threw to **wide receiver** Jimmy Smith.

Mark Brunell

Jimmy Smith

POCKET HERCULES

From 2006 to 2013, running back Maurice Jones-Drew was fast and powerful. People called him "Pocket Hercules" for his size and strength.

Running back Fred Taylor was hard to take down. He played 11 seasons with the Jaguars.

Tony Boselli was an anchor on **offense** from the team's beginning. Boselli was the first player **drafted** by the Jaguars. He played in the **Pro Bowl** five times.

Linebacker Daryl Smith on **defense** had a way of getting to the opponent's ball carrier. He had 537 career tackles for the Jaguars.

JAGUARS

TEAM GREATS

TONY BOSELLI
OFFENSIVE TACKLE
1995-2001

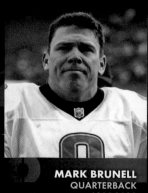

MARK BRUNELL
QUARTERBACK
1995-2003

JIMMY SMITH
WIDE RECEIVER
1995-2005

Tony
Boselli

FRED TAYLOR
RUNNING BACK
1998-2008

DARYL SMITH
LINEBACKER
2004-2012

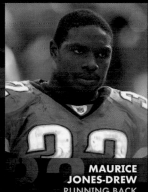

**MAURICE
JONES-DREW**
RUNNING BACK
2006-2013

23

Jacksonville is in Duval County. Fans chant a long "Duval" to distract the opposing team.

The Prowl is a Jaguars pregame tradition. When the Jaguars take the field, the fans line their path. Fans love getting close to the players.

4th quarter
bell

Another game tradition honors the United
States Armed Forces. A service member rings
a huge bell four times.

This bell begins the fourth quarter. With fun traditions and talented players, the Jaguars' fan base continues to grow. The team stays hot on the prowl for more winning seasons!

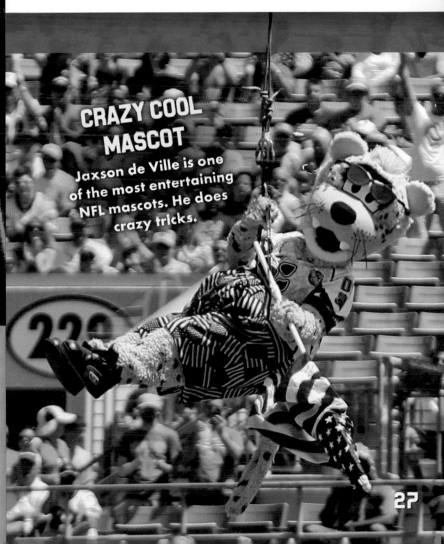

CRAZY COOL MASCOT

Jaxson de Ville is one of the most entertaining NFL mascots. He does crazy tricks.

Team name:
Jacksonville Jaguars

Team name explained:
**Named by fans during
a name-the-team contest**

Conference: AFC

Division: South

**Main rivals: Indianapolis Colts,
Tennessee Titans**

Joined NFL: 1995

Hometown:
Jacksonville, Florida

Training camp location: Florida Blue Health & Wellness Practice Fields, Jacksonville, Florida

JACKSONVILLE

FLORIDA

N
W + E
S

Home stadium name:
EverBank Field

Stadium opened: 1995

Seats in stadium: 67,246

Logo: A fierce jaguar head

Colors: Black, gold, teal

Mascot: Jaxson de Ville

GLOSSARY

conference—a large grouping of sports teams that often play one another

defense—the group of players who try to stop the opposing team from scoring

division—a small grouping of sports teams that often play one another; usually there are several divisions of teams in a conference.

drafted—chose a college athlete to play for a professional team

expansion teams—new teams added to a sports league

fumble—to lose the ball while it is still in play

linebacker—a player on defense whose main job is to make tackles and stop passes; a linebacker stands just behind the defensive linemen.

offense—the group of players who try to move down the field and score

playoffs—the games played after the regular NFL season is over; playoff games determine which teams play in the Super Bowl.

Pro Bowl—an all-star game played after the regular season in which the best players in the NFL face one another

quarterback—a player on offense whose main job is to throw and hand off the ball

rival—a long-standing opponent

running back—a player on offense whose main job is to run with the ball

sack—a play during which a player on defense tackles the opposing quarterback for a loss of yards

wide receiver—a player on offense whose main job is to catch passes from the quarterback

TO LEARN MORE

AT THE LIBRARY

Frisch, Nate. *The Story of the Jacksonville Jaguars.* Mankato, Minn.: Creative Education, 2014.

Stewart, Mark. *The Jacksonville Jaguars.* Chicago, Ill.: Norwood House Press, 2013.

Wyner, Zach. *Jacksonville Jaguars.* New York, N.Y.: AV2 by Weigl, 2015.

ON THE WEB

Learning more about the Jacksonville Jaguars is as easy as 1, 2, 3.

1. Go to www.factsurfer.com.

2. Enter "Jacksonville Jaguars" into the search box.

3. Click the "Surf" button and you will see a list of related web sites.

With factsurfer.com, finding more information is just a click away.

INDEX